DON'T BE SAD

Based on a True Story of Conquering Sadness

Author: Alton Edmond, Esquire

Illustrator: Michael Dunbar

D1157517

www.EdmondInspiration.com

Mission: To Proclaim Transformation and Truth
Publisher: Transformed Publishing, Cocoa, FL
Website: www.transformedpublishing.com
Email: transformedpublishing@gmail.com

Copyright © 2022 by Alton Edmond

Registration Number: TXu 2-337-229
Effective Date of Registration: September 12, 2022 / Registration Decision Date: October 05, 2022

Illustrations are property of Alton Edmond, created by Michael Dunbar.

All rights reserved solely by the author. No part of this book may be reproduced, stored in a retrieval system, or transmitted in any form or by any means without expressed written permission of the author.

This book is based on the author's personal experience and is not a recommended course of treatment for any mentioned life issues (relational, medical, mental, emotional, substance abuse, etc.). Names, characters, organizations, places, events, and incidents are used fictitiously to share the author's message.

ISBN: 978-1-953241-41-2

Acknowledgments:

To my babies Kaleb & Levi Wynn, Trinity & Lyla Edmond, and Myrrhiah Hatcher, I love you and whenever you feel sad, know I am here for you.

To Theresa Gray, Brenda Brooks, Georgia Coring, Sylvia Colley, Michael Irving, Jess Alford, Damarian Allen, Trae Martin, and Anthony Perkins, thank you for being part of my inspiration to rise from the fog that shrouded me once upon a time. Words cannot express how much I appreciate you.

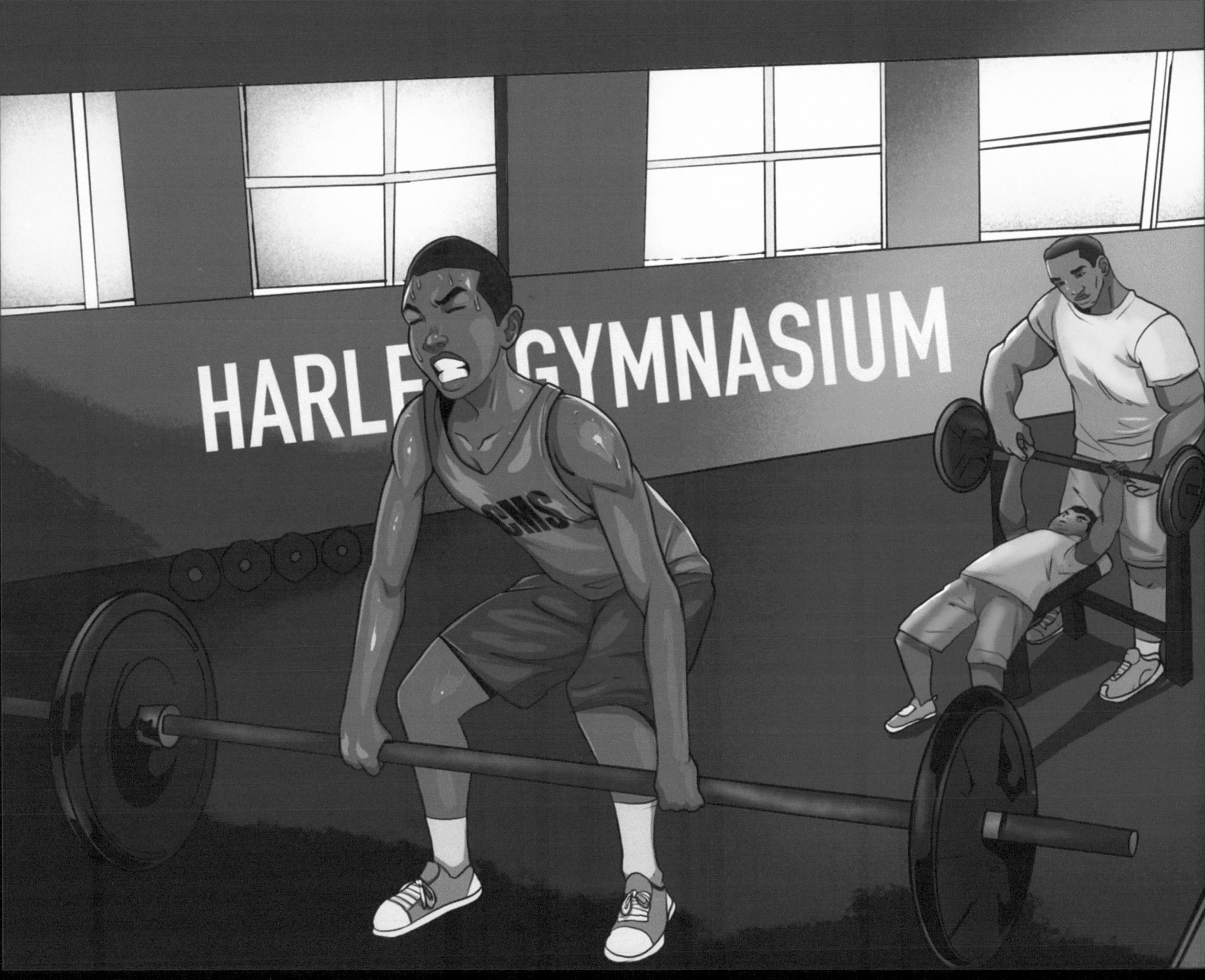
GYMNASIUM
CMS

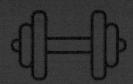

Alton does not have his
dad around to help
him lift heavy things.

This made Alton feel sad and powerless.

Alton often played alone because
he had no siblings or friends.

This made Alton feel sad and alone.

Alton had to wear clothes that were too big.
Sometimes his clothes were torn, too.
This was all his mom could afford.

This made Alton feel sad and embarrassed.

Thompson and the other kids laughed at Alton's clothes and called him names.

This made Alton feel sad and ashamed.

Winston took Alton's things and pushed him down at the playground.

This made Alton feel sad and afraid.

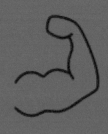

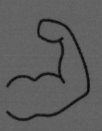

Coach Irving taught Alton how
to lift weights and he said,
"Don't be sad, I'll help you to be strong."

Trae and Mario invited Alton to play with them on the trampoline and they said, "Don't be sad, we will be your friends."

Tony gave Alton some of his nice clothes
that he did not wear anymore.
Tony said,
"Don't be sad, I'll help you dress to impress!"

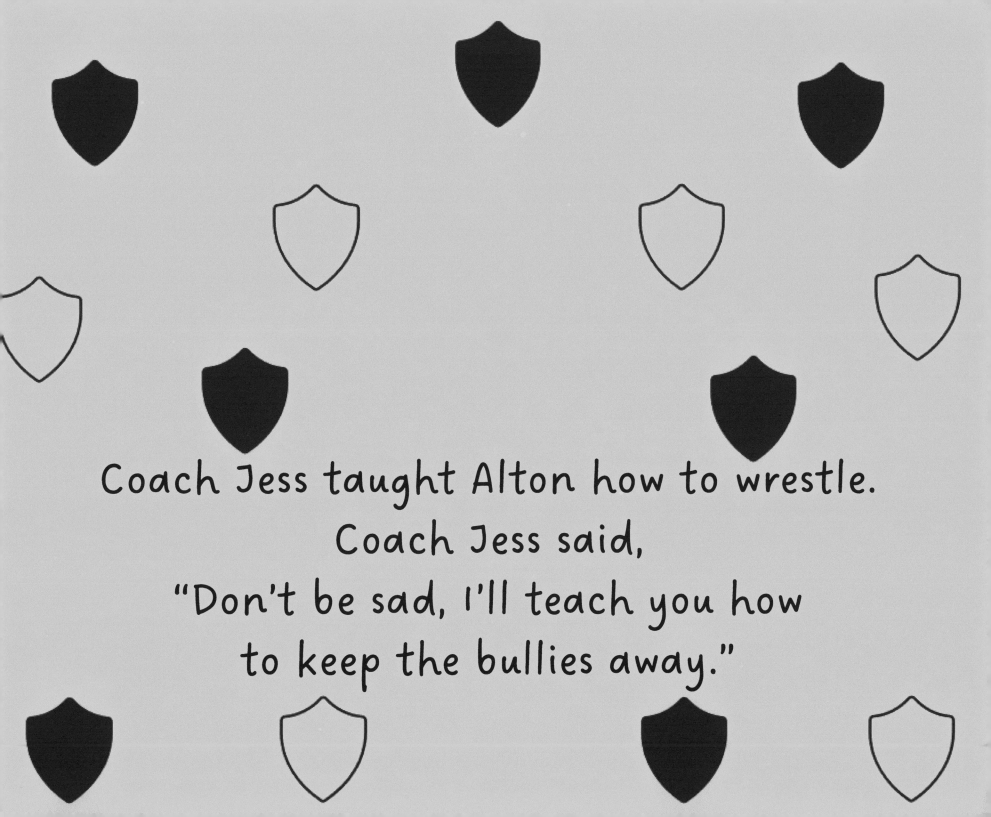

Coach Jess taught Alton how to wrestle.
Coach Jess said,
"Don't be sad, I'll teach you how
to keep the bullies away."

Alton feels strong now
that he can lift weights!

Alton does not feel alone now that he has friends to do fun things with.

CHS

Alton feels confident now that
he wears clothes that look nice.

Alton feels safe now that he can wrestle!

Alton feels happy and ready to take on whatever comes next!

<u>MESSAGE FROM THE AUTHOR</u>

This book is for anyone who has ever felt bad about themselves and wanted to quit. This book is for anyone who has ever disliked their life so much, it did not seem like there was much reason to continue. This book is for those who have been hurt and abused, even when they did nothing to deserve such treatment.

This book is about a very interesting time in my life. Interesting because of the challenges I faced, and the friends I gained in the process. I began this journey sad and depressed because I did not like myself or my life. I looked around and thought everyone had it better than I did. I later realized, even the most difficult times in life do not last. I also realized having the right people in your life helps change it for the better when you are ready for change. I battled with sadness, and I am glad I was ready for change.

I wrote this book to remind you, through my experiences, you can make it! Hold your head high. Today, I am an attorney, motivational speaker, real estate investor, community leader, coach, and philanthropist because I believed in myself. I believe in you. You can achieve anything you put your mind to. I encourage you to believe that too!

—Alton Terrance Edmond, Esquire

CPSIA information can be obtained
at www.ICGtesting.com
Printed in the USA
LVHW072013230223
740259LV00003B/91